Invasive Species Takeover

BURMESE PYTHONS

BARBARA CILETTI

BLACK
RABBIT
BOOKS

Bolt is published by Black Rabbit Books
P.O. Box 3263, Mankato, Minnesota, 56002.
www.blackrabbitbooks.com
Copyright © 2017 Black Rabbit Books

Design and Production by Michael Sellner
Photo Research by Rhonda Milbrett

Library of Congress Control Number: 2015954690

HC ISBN: 978-1-68072-017-4   PB ISBN: 978-1-68072-281-9

Printed in the United States at CG Book Printers,
North Mankato, Minnesota, 56003. PO #1793 4/16

Web addresses included in this book were working and appropriate at the time of publication. The publisher is not responsible for broken or changed links.

Image Credits
Barcroft India, Muller, 4–5;
biosphoto: Michel Gunther, 8-9;
Dreamstime: Oskari Porkka, 24; Flickr:
Camilla, 29; Chris Charlton, Cover; iStock:
konradlew, 21 (right); Newscom: Chris Brignell/
Photoshot, 28 (middle); Michael Barron/MCT,
6; St Petersburg Times/ZUMAPRESS, 23; Science
Source: John Mitchell, 3; Shutterstock: Anukool
Manoton, 32; cellistka, 20 (top), 31; Eric Isselee, 20
(both bottom); fivespots, 28 (bottom); Heiko Kiera,
10, 14, 15; IrinaK, 21 (middle); MP cz, 19; Paul Tes-
sier, 28 (top); Praisaeng, Back Cover, 1, 13; Robert
Eastman, 21 (left); Volt Collection, 26–27
Every effort has been made to contact copyright holders for material reproduced
in this book. Any omissions will be
rectified in subsequent printings
if notice is given to the
publisher.

Contents

CHAPTER 1

Chomped by a Snake

Scientists were working in the Florida Everglades in October 2005. Suddenly, they saw something they'd never seen before. They saw a dead alligator. And that alligator was sticking out of a snake!

Big Meal

The snake was a Burmese python. It had swallowed the alligator whole. Scientists aren't sure what happened next. Some think the snake burst open from that big meal.

Troubling Sight

The discovery of the snake and alligator was troubling. Scientists wondered what else the snakes were eating.

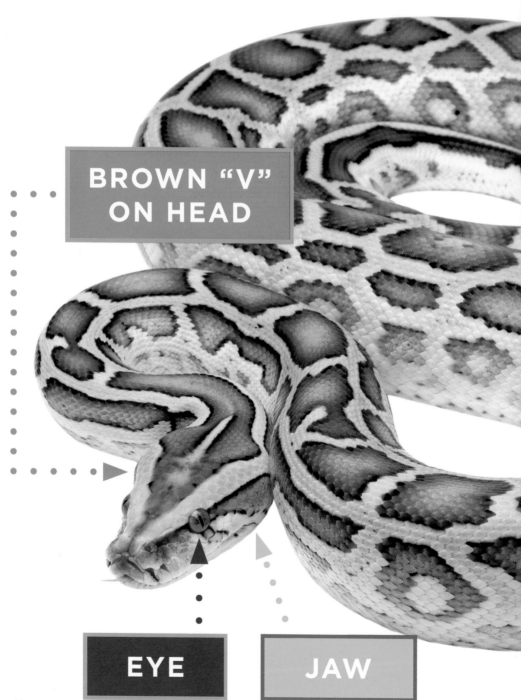

BROWN "V" ON HEAD

EYE

JAW

TAN AND DARK BROWN SPOTS

STOMACH

Invasive Species

Burmese pythons are not supposed to be in Florida. People brought them to the United States as pets. Some people then **released** the snakes into the wild. The snakes began to spread to new areas. They hurt the animals that already lived there. Burmese pythons are an **invasive species**.

CHAPTER 2

Not-So-Perfect

Burmese pythons are some of the biggest snakes on Earth. They come from southeast **Asia**. They live in jungles and grassy marshes.

People began bringing the snakes to the United States. They kept them as pets. But many didn't realize how big their pets could get. An adult python can be 20 feet (6 meters) long or more.

Released in the Wild

Many owners couldn't handle the snakes' big size. They dumped their snakes in the wild. Many people left their snakes in Everglades National Park (ENP).

The pythons are **predators**. They easily hid in tall grasses. They ate any animals they could trap. And they began to lay eggs. Few predators eat the snakes. So the population grew.

WHERE BURMESE PHYTHONS COULD SPREAD

Yes

Maybe

No

Canada

WHERE BURMESE
PHYTHONS ARE NOW

Established   Possible

United States

Mexico

CHAPTER 3

Big Trouble

Today, pythons are causing trouble in the ENP. No one knows how many are in the park. These snakes are taking food other animals need. Some animals have to find new homes. Others starve to death.

BURMESE PYTHON

DEER

BOBCAT

Eaten Up

Some animals in the ENP are **endangered**. That means few of them are left. Pythons are eating these animals. The snakes could make some animals go **extinct**.

ALLIGATOR

RABBIT

SQUIRREL

CHAPTER 4

Stopping the Snakes

Scientists are looking for ways to stop the snakes. They have put **tracking devices** on some pythons. Then they watch where the snakes go. They hope to learn how the snakes live. That information could help them stop the animals.

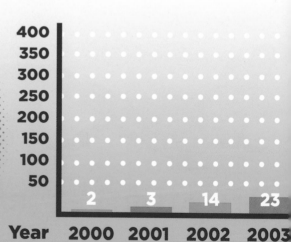

Pythons Removed from Everglades National Park

Year	2000	2001	2002	2003
	2	3	14	23

70	94	170	248	343	367	322	169	152
2004	2005	2006	2007	2008	2009	2010	2011	2012

Tracking and Trapping

Researchers are trying to use dogs and traps too. Dogs can be trained to smell the snakes. Some people think dogs can help find the sneaky snakes.

Scientists are also testing traps to catch pythons. They put a female snake's scent on the trap. Then males come to the trap, looking for a mate.

Stopping Trouble

Burmese pythons are troublemakers. They are changing the **ecosystem** in the ENP. If they're not stopped, they could spread. These slithering snakes could invade other places. And they could do a lot of damage.

BURMESE PYTHONS BY THE NUMBERS

16 to 23
FEET
(5 to 7 meters)

average length

EGGS A FEMALE
CAN LAY AT
ONE TIME

UP TO
200
POUNDS
(91 kilograms)

weight

20 to 25
YEARS

average
life span

Think

about It. . .

1. People brought Burmese pythons to the United States. Should people be allowed to bring animals to other countries? Explain why or why not.

2. Endangered animals live in the ENP. Use other sources to find out what animals live in the park.

3. Burmese pythons are actually endangered animals in Asia. Could there be benefits to having the snakes in the United States? Why or why not?

Asia (A-zhuh)—a continent in the eastern hemisphere

ecosystem (E-co-sys-tum)—a community of living things in one place

endangered (in-DAYN-jurd)—close to becoming extinct

extinct (ek-STINGKT)—no longer existing

invasive species (in-VAY-siv SPEE-seez)—animals or plants that spread through an area where they are not native, often causing problems for native plants and animals

predator (PRED-uh-tuhr)—an animal that eats other animals

release (re-LEES)—to allow a person or animal to leave a jail or cage

tracking device (TRA-king de-VIYS)—a piece of equipment that uses GPS to show the location of something

LEARN MORE

Aronin, Miriam. *Florida's Burmese Pythons: Squeezing the Everglades.* They Don't Belong: Tracking Invasive Species. New York: Bearport Publishing, 2016.

Oachs, Emily Rose. *Burmese Pythons.* Amazing Snakes! Minneapolis: Bellwether Media, 2014.

Spilsbury, Richard. *Invasive Reptiles and Amphibian Species.* Invaders from Earth. New York: PowerKids Press, 2015.

WEBSITES

Burmese Pythons
www.nps.gov/ever/learn/nature/ burmesepythonsintro.htm

Invasion of the Giant Pythons
www.pbs.org/wnet/nature/invasion-of-the-giant- pythons-introduction/5532/

Nonnatives —Burmese Python
myfwc.com/wildlifehabitats/nonnatives/reptiles/ burmese-python/

INDEX